TURNING ON THE WASP

Poems by Rob Azevedo

Kung Fu Treachery Press
Rancho Cucamonga, CA

Copyright ©Rob Azevedo, 2020
First Edition: 1 3 5 7 9 10 8 6 4 2
ISBN: 978-1-952411-38-0
LCCN: 2020951596

Cover photo: Rob Azevedo
Author photo: AJ Kierstead
All rights reserved. No part of this publication may be reproduced or transmitted in any form or by any means, electronic or mechanical, including photocopying, recording or by info retrieval system, without prior written permission from the author.

Acknowledgments:

Other places these poems ran: *Gasconade Review, Rye Whiskey Review, Cajun Mutt Press* and *allpoetry.com*

TABLE OF CONTENTS

SNAGGLE TOOTH / 1

VELVET WALLS / 2

THE BLUES AIN'T DEAD! / 4

WHERE I BELONG / 5

I CAN'T WAIT / 6

TRAPPED IN A VERSE / 7

SUFFOCATING ON GUILT / 8

THE WANING LIGHT OF DAWN / 9

BROKEN BOILS / 10

FOGGED OVER / 11

BLINDING, HEAPING, BEGGING, BLAMING / 13

LORD SWEATY MOUTH / 14

SUCKING AT THE BONE / 15

JOUSTING FOR MERCY / 16

BOWLS OF WRATH / 17

STAUNCH FORGIVENESS / 18

GRUMBLING FIENDS / 19

GNAWING BUZZARDS / 20

WITCHES ON BENT BROOMS / 22

ELECTRIC SKIRT (FOR IGGY POP) / 23

NEVER AGAIN / 24

CLUTCH THE KNOT / 25

QUEST TO BE HEARD / 26

OCD AND ME / 27

HOUNDS OF MERCY / 28

SILENCE! / 29

GONE UPTOWN / 30

MARCO! POLO! / 32

VOMITIOUS DAYS / 33

DANCING WITH SWINE / 35

TYING OFF THE TIP / 36

WAVES OF LOVE / 37

TURNING ON THE WASP / 38

YOU SEE ME / 39

PLAYLIST / 41

STEP INTO THE BOX / 42

DIRTY SPARROW / 43

RATS! / 44

THE LEDGES / 45

STILL BURNING / 46

FRANK / 47

LOVE BEFORE DEATH / 49

TREACHEROUS / 50

THE JERSEY FLASH / 51

COZY / 52

JUST THIS BOX / 53

NIGHT BREAKS AGAINST THE PUPIL / 54

BRAIDED TONGUES / 55

PAWING AT THE WAVES / 56

NIGHT ANGELS / 57

THE THING ABOUT COURAGE / 58

For Buk

*If it doesn't burst out of you
in spite of everything,
don't do it.*

-Charles Bukowski

SNAGGLE TOOTH

Two sour-faced virgins
lap at the wet mud
beneath their dirty feet,
cursing the snaggle-toothed gentry,
all covered in scabs
and boils
and liver spots,
fast asleep
under the bridge
wrapped in rags,
on a starless night
consumed with gas
with spite
with sperm
during a pandemic
and brag about their purity.

VELVET WALLS

Escape we must
from the velvet walls of eternity
dashing souls past matted earth
and dried roses
propped as bed sheets upon
our death sacks
with slouched shoulders we crouch
our hungry bones
our sunken cheeks
our borrowed teeth
our braided tongues
we jam a life
into this barren cave
left only to feed off
ourselves
now hollowed bodies of
membrane
bacteria
and the bitter cells of our past
choking at the roots of creation
beautifully rotting in symphony
dreaming the same dream
swimming alone
along the same seas
among the same fields
forever and beyond
for our task now is to

follow the sounds
of the revelers above us
dancing among the stones
with words of allegiance
while the harboring gale winds
burn at the salty tears billowing
off the familiar powdered jaws
of lovers come and gone
each more radiant
saddened to a point
soon rush off for one last gasp
one last memory
before the grapes wrinkle
before the sun sleeps
before the winds cut close
where all that's left is to lick at the walls
of worn velvet
gathering dust with all the others
soon long forgotten.

THE BLUES AIN'T DEAD!

Penniless, from the crowded stage
the yellow-eyed blues man
sets off rockets with his red guitar
as the tangled wino's huddle
over small glasses of rye
and pick at each others teeth
as the short order cooks stare
longingly at the tramps backstage
lined up to swallow tongues
while the valet stacks lines of powder
on some strangers dash
and plugs his nose
cursing the skies shouting,
"The Blues Ain't Dead!"
"The Blues Ain't Dead!"

WHERE I BELONG

feel like flippin' a quarter
catchin' it in my dirty palm
thick with railroad grease
on the back roads,
where I belong.

feel like jumpin' rails
stompin' on some toothless bums
shake em' down for pennies,
where I belong.

feel like kickin' in some barn doors
settlin' down in a bed of straw
dreamin' of dreams long forgotten,
where I belong.

feel like cracking open a can of beans
washin' my face in a puddle of mud
singin' some chain-gang songs with my filthy cohorts,
where I belong.

feel like slidin' into a new town
pretendin' to be anything but what I am
cozyin' up to something warm and sweet,
right where I belong.

I CAN'T WAIT

Unless the mud is soaked like hot flowing lava,
I can't wait.
Unless the rich are filled with grace and spirit,
I can't wait.
Unless the poor are fed and considered,
I can't wait.
Unless the proud are graceful in their adoration,
I can't wait.
Unless the mountains rise with the burning sun,
I can't wait.
Unless love blooms across a nation divided,
I can't wait.
Unless pride is restored in the minds of the wicked,
I can't wait.
Unless peace is sprung upon vicious minds,
I can't wait.
Unless forgiveness is granted to those who sin,
I can't wait.
Unless gratitude is bestowed upon those who sacrificed with honor,
I can't wait.

Unless....well, I just can't wait.

TRAPPED IN A VERSE

I kept saying to myself
this phase will end,
that the phantom beneath the mask
who bore great resemblance
to the coward condemned to mediocrity
survived trapped in the same verse,
the same song,
the same poem,
who immerged to deliver
great bouts of clarity,
jaunty caravans of inspiration
layered with wonder,
constricted by none,
delegated to suffer,
yet the masked impersonator
lingered about on the fringes,
spouting cryptic slang,
stumbling at art,
then finally,
and with great haste,
bowed to the ranks
of finks and frauds.

SUFFOCATING ON GUILT

The body drips with guilt, writhing on the insides,
housing a nothingness which smolders
with crooked smile as the knife digs deeper into the
unchanged ways.

The mind drowns in guilt, suffocating on traits
long lost on promise, the hinderance flows
like a sour patch of bruised apples falling
towards nowhere.

The skin aches from guilt, jarred with knots which
tighten in the dark, my toes shed skin as the sky
drizzles stones and measures my contempt
for honesty.

The heart pumps with guilt, butchering each organ
with sweltering heat that fades beneath the truth
clawing at my ribcage, bellowing for each regret
to track its reckless abandonment.

The eyes sting with guilt, blinded by the caustic
shame smashing against each doorframe,
sending bloodless murmurs to protect the lies
which orbit the echoes of my wrong doings.

THE WANING LIGHT OF DAWN

One lung fills with crusty blades of grass,
soiled quietly by the dim light of dawn.

One eye waves goodbye to the squandered angels,
their blackened wings now twisted across a swollen pelvis.

One tooth shades the next, broken away
from the limbs of God, softened by aching skies.

One toe digs in the supple earth, content to hide
beneath the devastating wane of decency.

One heart burns with exception, once a blooming
bolt of humanity now shattered by a raging underworld.

One finger swipes at thick, hot tears, bitter from ruminating
on a universe centered on domination.

One hand cups the next, meshed together in solidarity
as the husky skyline cranes its neck to reach the horizon.

One-foot kicks at the heavens, clever in its trickery,
as hope drowns in a muddy river of laughter and despair.

One lung, one eye, one tooth, a toe, the heart, a finger,
hand and foot, each shattered by an unending wake of
ignorance trembling with disease.

BROKEN BOILS

she was aging out
barely holding on
to her looks
but she had some spark left
in her eyes
but her breath was vile
hot and sticky
and she was always picking
at her crooked teeth
which smelled like fish
and she was covered in boils
which broke open during heatwaves
and her skin was coated
in smoke stains
but there was life in her yet
she was a lousy poet
she read some good books
and she had cash and always
bought the beer and
she let me sleep on her couch
when I was too drunk
so I kept her around
for a few weeks
and put up with her breath
and boils
and bent teeth
and tired words.
because she always bought the beer.

FOGGED OVER

The glint in my eye fogs over
as the meat of my hands
begin to rumble.

The rustling started in my chest, that
rambling, hollow, slow rolling emotion
that stinks of disease, trucked its way into
my elbows and neck, which has tightened
as each minute of the show clicks by.

Ruined by the human condition,
exhausted with lust, these trumpets
spit blood at the hungry crowd,
baiting the savages to widen
their tongues.

For blood, for revenge, for sport.
The rich, the brooding, the warped
scramble like hounds to cry into
the eyes of each victim, scorched
and torn with cruel intention.

The taste of dead fish captures
my senses, that ruinous aftertaste
melds its way into my candor, lacing
the hours in knotted anxiousness.

It's all too much -- the betrayal,
the contempt, the flaming minds
that swell with indifference.

BLINDING, HEAPING, BEGGING, BLAMING

the governing masses with delinquent minds
throw sawdust in the naked eye of nature
blinding us wildly into hysteria
heaping chunky bit of bile onto our baffled minds
hanging slogans on our precious trees
blaming madness on angry mobs
demoralizing demonstrators
vilifying the media
redefining our genders
systematically defacing our pleasures
shunning poverty for profit
rising only to meet the fears they breed
as they beg us to drink from their vicious cups
overflowing with greed and power.

LORD SWEATY MOUTH

Tyranny, that is what I imagined upon meeting you.
That you were a tyrant with open-mouth sores.
Your face smelled of old crust, deeply lined and gray,
as if plowed over with a dull blade.

Your breath was hot, fuming from yesterday's feast
as you bent over me, pen in hand, ready to castrate
my creation with stained fingernails twisted in smoke.

I feared that you would expose me for the hack I am,
a phony, a fraud, someone less than worthy of starvation.

Then, with your sweaty mouth and yellow fingers,
you assured me that I belonged among the peasants,
those wretched minds bent on fabrication.

Cautiously, you freed my jugular of raw indignation
and drew a path along the braided wires
that crossed between hope and salvation,
guiding me on bulletproof vapors,
shattering all doubts birthed from a cryptic mind.

SUCKING AT THE BONE

Mutants abound boarding
vessels of indignation
burrow sideways with watchful eyes,
debating fragments of lies,
lavishly longing
beyond the wall of truth
with plumes of rank,
of file,
of vile hypocrisy,
craving only
cheap sentiment
and lawless prayer
sent and shaped
with hook and horn,
sucking at the bones of democracy
as the dawn curls back into midnight.

JOUSTING FOR MERCY

Together we ride on flaming wings
Into the coiled underworld, gulping
At the embers which chock our existence.
Our calves empty of blood
Our toes scratch and twitch at the earth's
Fading floor as we rush headlong
Into the gallows, dressed in our Sunday best.

The lawless hunter which stole our souls
Now masks our eyes with matted hair
As the river beyond cries songs of mercy.
My sister, blinded and weightless, sways
In the gray autumn sound, now filled with echo's
Of the ignorant, gagging on our choices,
Ruined without love, docked for life
In these septic woods, jousting for mercy.

BOWLS OF WRATH

Shamelessly vacant
with bow-legged gait,
hollow in sound
but for eyes caste wide
in silence,
the panther draws blood
from hungry cries
smoldering for verbiage unknown.

Feeding the raving fiends
bold lies to feast upon
at dusk with oily lips
hanging powerless
beneath crusted bowls of wrath
they hop and gallop
'round deadly prose,
sucking at the air,
baiting the fireflies, shouting,
"The deadlier the line, the better!"

STAUNCH FORGIVENESS

The smoky-eyed combustible gaze
falling across the young boy's face
is rewarded with staunch forgiveness,
leveling his uncertainties towards truth,
stirring his doubts with rings of hope.

Whist the wayward son's determination
rekindles with each passing reward,
steeling his weighted courage with
blessings where his shadow dawns
on bulging light.

As he travels through life
with haughty delight,
knowing that wolves bite and walls fall,
unbroken nor exhausted, the boy stares deep
into the hazy sky above,
propelling past each hesitation.

GRUMBLING FIENDS

Wince like the filthy pagan beast you are,
sharpened against the rot that corrodes
your cursed libido.

Laughter follows you with mockery,
greasing the wheels of your fragmented mind,
blessed with hardened dung,
layered in unforgivable lust.
Isolated with a hollow soul,
the Lord stretches out before you barefooted
with shiv in hand, pointing you towards
the doors of damnation.

You have danced amongst the sleeping hearts,
the grumbling fiends fixed on insatiable nights,
lost in nylon and oils and images
of the rank, the vile, a mid-morning
spectacle of staggering deviance.

You have lost yourself.

Now, bow to the shiv.

Honor your penance.

This will only take a minute.

GNAWING BUZZARDS

Untouched for too long,
an island all your own,
you shaped your days
around a thorny, splintered
gaze, hellbent on self-mutilation.

Lamenting the uncontrollable,
the chest heaves and gulps
at the buzzards gnawing at
your burning thoughts, crouched
against the wall of shame.

We watched you crumble
beneath natures lying eyes,
clouded over in a body of
defiance angled towards
destruction.

The mystery deepens on fallen winds,
leaving lovers and friends speechless,
clueless in their desperate attempts
to govern your spirit, a blazing palace
of moral confusion.

Expectations unattainable,
the margins collapse around
earths fragile moon beams,

we call on you to rise up and
set fire to heaven and hell,
kiss the image you were birthed,
and mock the days
in which you suffer.

WITCHES ON BENT BROOMS

Scary for only so long,
soon you will whimper beyond
the patches which warmed
your short future.

The crown on your head is softening,
blackened in spots, rotting
alongside the ghouls, ghosts
and witches bent on begging brooms.

Your sweet tooth aches,
thorny fingers bend,
crooked smile deadened
in the hot autumn sun.

I stare at your disjointed elbow
and my own teeth crack and fall
into my gum line, struggling to reach
the cocoa boiling beneath your powered
fingers.

Dust me with sugar,
coat me in an orange glow,
bury me with the seeds that
sow fear and dread.

ELECTRIC SKIRT (FOR IGGY POP)

Seemingly translucent,
a gyrating roll of telephonic proportions,
Iggy writhes lizard-like with cork screw
feathers stealing kisses
with his electric stench fuming from
stampeding speed heads
crashing violently against the stage,
bellowing for the Ig to Pop
and cut himself with razorblades
as their mouths lay agape --
blending time with madness --
eager to lap at the lustful life
hidden beneath his ironed skirt.

NEVER AGAIN

The flowing gown of our
barren past lays in ruin beneath
broken shells of skin and bone,
evading all love, will, hope, desire
-- the crux of our faded glory --
for I claim you
only to lose you,
and love you
only to watch you burn
as my spine rips
and blackheads burst
across my knees, screaming,
"Never again! Never!"

Until the next time.

CLUTCH THE KNOT

Blather and boast
as a heroic knight
in your tin can rags and
powdered feathers as
you clutch at your boneless knot
with a skinless smirk
doubting the might
of all damnation
while castrating
the barkers for barking
the doers for doing
the lovers for loving
all against your will
as your pasty lips rise
thick with promises never kept
swinging that soft cock
at empty skies.

QUEST TO BE HEARD

Listless beyond recognition,
the Greasehead pounds away
with invisible might
with paws of clay
with firm intent
chasing a dream only he can
see through a prism
of reverence and hope
as the Lord set fire to his fingertips
he savagely tugs at the morning
now basting in a rancid hue
he claws at the truth
which lays
beyond his overwhelming
need to be heard.

OCD AND ME

Claustrophobic in my containment,
I buckle my belt and pull at my socks
with darting eyes fixated on formality.

Scrubbing down on faded fingernails,
I work to free the dirt from its proper form
until my skin boils with cleanliness.

The turning face of a clock never ending,
its body lingers and swats at the closing night
as my heart thumps and clogs with visions of delirium.

My unwashed mind careens against a braided fence
housing my obsessions as I linger towards
a crowded mass of haughty torment, blazing my libido.

The witch doctor prays upon my weakened state,
branding me corrupted, lost and dissolved as fate
seals the edges of manic fright, now burning tales of
black magic.

Plumes of garbage masquerad as treasures lost,
consume my days, violently angling for my attention
as a volcanic urge weightlessly fades till dawn.

The more I touch, find, finger and collect, the longer
my exhausting purpose masks itself as a miracle.

HOUNDS OF MERCY

Shards of glass capped in white
whisk and bend at the soggy walls
soon wading in the currents
beneath the armored blackened skies
as live wires swat at calming hands,
mocking the filthy, the petulant, the loyal,
their laughter now drowning with little gain
as nature hushes at the angels perched
along rooftops on the shore, praying
to the hounds with curled speech for mercy.

SILENCE!

Now, the weeks go by and it is what it is.

A new beginning, the "New Normal."

A much-needed trimming of the fat maybe.

The bloat we have carried for two decades has had its say.

We have gorged our faces.

Stuffed our guts. Seduced our egos.

And none of us are innocent of this profound sense of neediness.

The phone, the posts, the face grabs,

The mangled, manicured pool-side toe shots,

The texts, the updates, the long lines of staged cleavage.

Now! Now! Now! I Want It Now!

That constant in-your-face means of communication

High in volume, low in substance

Well, she bit back and left bloody teeth marks.

Now, silence! All of us!

GONE UPTOWN (FOR JUSTIN TOWNES EARLE)

He's gone uptown, the lanky wizard,
inked from wrist to ear,
dogged no more
in bloodline tears,
wound tighter than a corkscrew.

From the bowels of burden,
notoriously bred
tiger red in his veins,
young son mines his way
through damp-skinned nights
rose up with Fender-laced frame.

The gallows of youth bore might,
bowls of girth and haste,
a voice all its own,
strong yet alone,
cursed over with thunderous flight.

His fingers flew once
with the arc of sawdust,
plucked sweet off Delta din floors.
He traveled, he sang,
with a grand middle name,
never far from deaths front door.

His music too miss,
a long nasal kiss,
the River of Harlem shines bright
along the shore.

MARCO! POLO!

Marco!
Polo!
Marco!
Polo!
Marco!
Polo!

With that, I take to the shallow end
and cut wide strides,
shouldering my way
through the chemical bubbles,
my nylon suit riding high up my backside,
I approach the deep end as
the merchant once did Genoa,
with humility, not haste,
and I dash past the smooth naked thighs
of unattainable hip bones,
writhing with desire,
bursting at the lungs,
eyes whipped about with each deep stroke,
burning long and lasting,
each adventurer diving deep
into the depth of our travels,
trading silk, exotic plants, and gunpowder
along the way, masking our fears
with an emperor's stare,
living to see another day.

VOMITIOUS DAYS

That little girl's tears are screaming,
and the boy, the one who is not old
enough to grow hair on his arms,
his innards are enflamed with terror.

The eyes on that toddler, the one
in the baby blue shirt gripping the cage
with one-inch fingers that are now
turning blue, his heart is crying,
day and night, night and day,
for Mama.

Those two sisters, the ones with bare feet
and dark circles under their eyes, they
were just cornered by four teenaged boys,
bent on taking their anger out on someone.

That sad-eyed son of a farmer, the one
in the corner alone, staring into a nightmare
only he can see, he might live to kiss his parents
again, but for now they too are caged,
or banished to their homeland,
childless and broken.

That nine-year old girl wearing a loose
ponytail in dirty hair, holding a screaming baby
in her arms that stinks of week-old feces,
her life as a child is over before it started.

A child raising a child.

And I could go on.

But I want to vomit writing this.

So, I will not.

DANCING WITH SWINE

Oh, to dance among the swine
on this gruesome night
with hollowed legs
swinging wildly possessed
as church bells roar midnight
across the barren weed fields
off Lola Ave.

Gripping onto the night as if
your darkest secrets really mattered,
you peek into the slits of your future
and moan achingly at the stars --
cursing them for their intentions --
for it is they who strangled you
with deaths dark shadows.

Leaning now against fading light
with shuttered eyes crusted over --
morning begins to turn on its side --
you spit at the sleepy-eyed hogs
in the dewy fields reciting Jeffers
and the sweaty cows quoting Hughes
and the lonely children
licking at the salty tears
once cried by Sylvia,
as you bathe in the fleshless
gaze of salvation.

TYING OFF THE TIP

whining fiend, all clogged
with lust, consumed with scented
nylon and aged cleavage,
moans while his swollen member
bends and begs to be released
from its impulsive urges.
The brute sulks impatiently,
then ties off the tip,
cringing in each bone,
weak with fantasy, and
saves his batch for another day.

WAVES OF LOVE

Shoeless, maybe,
with only cotton in his pockets,
a rowdy toenail hanging
awkwardly from out of a sandal
once worn
by his vagrant uncle,
he slides headlong
into the tide as dusk fades
in slants across his bookish
ass, now damp with sand
from the Atlantis breakers.

You study his determined grin as he
mounts his sled and
gasps for fresh breath, pounding
at the current, his mouth
washed with salt, his bulbous
nose thrashed in the cutting sea,
as you wait and watch
curling your toes into the sand,
throbbing on the inside,
ready to burst from
the roll-and-tumble
gripping your belly and heart,
riding hard on the wave of love.

TURNING ON THE WASP

From the gallows I emerge
dwarfed by fading grace,
pawing at earth's cruel conscience,
unwilling, at first, to counter
the swarming
wasps sucking
at my fragile dome,
needling my eyes
with venomous stout.

Eager to break from the chains
of indulgence, I soon turn
on the wasp,
pinning its chocking greed
to a bloody cross stained with
the sin of my father,
draining the heathen
of its flaming footprints
as it sinks underfoot
back into the earth,
wingless
and diseased.

YOU SEE ME

All you rank strangers
dragged and whipped about,
you don't deserve my tears,
they will boil first before I
set gaze upon your broken
smile as you whisper
and hint at my rotten luck.

You see the birthmarks of
my sins, the scars that flame
from my bloodless arms,
my buckled knees, my chinless
jaw, you see!

You see me faded
out, licking the curb at midnight,
fighting the nod as quarters
fly faceless into the ruined gutter
beneath my empty cup.

You see me there
in your nightmares,
fighting back rusted tears,
chasing you beyond the trees
while you plow the earth
with my battered face.

Oh, you see me!

But you will not see my tears.

They are only mine to taste.

PLAYLIST

The harbored face of a grieving father
with eyes smothered in vengeance
stands alone,
rolled over by countless sleepless nights,
untether to any beloved creator
but One
finds solace in the old playlists once
crafted with love
in jazz, in hip-hop, in indie and pop,
a roller coaster of rhythm,
tracking from melody to word
from word to harmony
across his redwood arms,
with winks of light bursting thick
like worms beneath his branded
marks of misery,
he tries to squeeze
new life out each beat,
welded into each song,
working to pump out the darkness
while pleading to his baby girl,
his One creator,
to please come home.

STEP INTO THE BOX

Wash down your mirror, brother,
and make it shine bright again,
for the light in your eyes has vanished
and done warped your vision
of right and wrong.

Step into the box, son, and get
right with God, whomever that may be.
Spill your sins then wash your face
with lawless tears. Mumble clearly then
seal your faith with a legion of godly prayers.

Bring your ego to a halt, sister,
burn it out of yourself and knock it
back into its rightful place.
Hordes of haters will love you
for your calming presence
now plucked and trimmed and
properly approachable.

Call on the people you left, father,
the little tykes with runny noses,
buckled thoughts and caustic manners,
needing only a beefy shoulder to
lean on and a steady heart to trust.

Then turn the page and move on.

DIRTY SPARROW

Battered to-and-fro,
left to languish
upon a bed of burning coals,
the flaming-eyed sparrow would
arrive late at night,
long after the bedded beauties had
burrowed deep into a long nights slumber,
the sparrow and I would joust
for position -- he fighting to feast
on my soul, as I would unravel
my crippled chain of defense
and whip at his fiery eyes, his
toxic claws with desperation.

For the sparrow tempted and teased,
working to seduce my languishing disposition,
eager to persecute me for my proven weaknesses,
yet, soon, the hunter was hunted
as I waited in sleep, filled with remorse,
stained in crimson, I would slash and heap
horror on the sparrow, for the sparrow was just
that, a mere bird, while I, the pursued,
struck back with the force of a thousand angry crows
and burned its blackened wings
in a pit of gasoline, engulfed in flames as
I slid towards the next nightmare to conquer.

RATS!

I see them too
scurrying below my feet
within these caged walls
sucking at my sores
my nose hairs
my crusted lips
they surround me
eager to pounce on my fears
my crushed existence
my cellmates bleeding tattoos
all that I have left...gone
with no cheese
or cheer
or love to share
just time and sweat and failure
to communicate within these
detention walls.

For if I scream, I die.

THE LEDGES

You wore only brown skin
a nudists paradise
cut rocks and tiny beaches.
Basking in the sun,
hiding from what is right,
my dented skin trembled as
I looked at you -- aching, wishing, craving.

You fed me a smile
then turned away.

STILL BURNING

she ran her eyes across mine
with legs shining of burnt oil
a buttock built out of bedrock
with toes cuts like diamonds
painted a red shovel glow
digging
deep into flowing loins
battered about wall-to-wall
by waves of dizziness
cresting with lust
bulging with desire
beyond proper
and
owned by buttery skin
her whip-locked hair
her balloon lips lying
owning my thoughts
my vices
my haughty ways

so, i slunk away, half a man
and closed my eyes
dreamed of oils and rocks and shovels
then slept in sweat, still burning.

FRANK

It's not often
that I'm awoken by my screaming wife
as I peel my hungover face
from the pillow
my sticky tongue off the floor
only to look out my window
to find a homeless man
sleeping in my backyard
curled up next to a fallen dead tree.

Bloody from his own sullied ways
lost in the brush
far from home,
from anything familiar
a stampede of sadness in his eyes
carrying only a bag of frozen pizzas
and little memory
of his past
or his drowning future.

Frank shakes the crusted leaves
off his chipped knees
the blood from his old wrists
the dirt off his crooked teeth
and together we ride around town

both beat to shit
exhausted by life
torn open from the long night
and go in search
of anything recognizable.

LOVE BEFORE DEATH

a single checkered cab emerges
from the steamy streets of Times Square
swallowed up with hate and fear
as the radio cracks under pressure
and the winos scamper to collect soggy cigarettes
and the hookers pull at their torn, dirty panties
and the bloated businessman stumbles drunkenly
into the backseat, blacked out and lonely
as the hustlers tap at their fedoras
pushing their filth on the weak
while the dead-eyed cabbie scans the square
for prey, for love, for companionship
and emerges from the steam mohawked
and desperate for redemption
terrified of his own thoughts --
each more violent than the next
crying out for love before death.

TREACHEROUS

the treacherous hump weighed down
with beefy neck, feigning spurs, calling
hate love
light dark
pain peace
gimping about on legless breath
harnessing the populous with viciousness
as they lap down on his fiery bowls
of mouth water
saliva bleeding
gums rotting
teeth cracked with grease
and tainted eggs --
nothing to behold
no hope or aspiration
just blasphemy and contempt
a kingdom of lies that burn, burn, burn
as the nation
tears at skin and the mangled ways
of a generation long past
buried beneath the poisonous
slumping and moaning
for true love
something of which he knows nothing of
and never will.

THE JERSEY FLASH

Carved out of a John Ford movie
crusted and torn to perfection
his forearms speak of strength
his lyrics of muscle and hope
undaunted by age
unflappable in his intentions
The Jersey Flash growls
with the angels at night
and sings
for the desperate
for the lost
for the forsaken
then rides off into the Badlands
screaming,
"Is there anybody alive out there!"

COZY

In the warmth
of the sheets
of my own bed,
I wish to lie
like a fetus
until I'm dead.

JUST THIS BOX

We need nothing more
this and only this
joined and everlasting
our fates reborn on shallow moons
waving alone at no one
lashed and crowned
the earth between each kiss
damp with pined grooved tongue
our breath, the air, the fasting
deliberate and abandoned
we need nothing more.

Just this box

NIGHT BREAKS AGAINST THE PUPIL

I see the day roll out before me,
behind me, above me.

I see the night break against my pupils,
plump and wet and lazy.

I see the dawn of a new generation
branded beyond recognition.

I touch the moonlight carrying me
on ribbons of silver and gold.

I hear the sounds of yearning,
compounded with greed and weakness.

I see the shadows of my past
lending shame to each twitching wink.

I feel the weight of traitors tested
and muzzled against the tide of denial.

I blink at each nightmare crowding
my jumbled sleep with fear and defeat.

I shout at each deepening bowl of fury,
empty of sunlight and hope.

I sense the break of dawn crawling
up my spine, addressing the day before me.

BRAIDED TONGUES

Cut clean from God's rich intent,
we bandy about on braided tongues
whispering at the unearthed mysteries
afforded to us to figure out,
to surmise with stylish contemplation,
each of us crucified on widowed
wounded wings,
gasping for the truth,
harking back at the empty sky
to deliver a judgement upon us
as we languish in a mote of
godless confusion.

PAWING AT THE WAVES

She paws at the waves
crashing in on her
foamed faced and
buried in the salt and sweat
of the roaring sea,
crusader of none,
alone in her wild splendor,
gasping at the ruins
as she shimmers in the
far off fading sun,
waiting for the sea
to swallow her toes.

NIGHT ANGELS

I don't know much about
angels.

Every time I pray to one,
I wake up with a raw red
nose.

Looking like Rudolph.

Never figured out why.
Maybe it's the content, the
way I pray and all.

No couth. No commitment.

Feathered silence, always.

But, I don't quit.

I keep screwing up and praying to them angels
every night
hoping someday I'll hear them
praying back.

Getting tired of this raw nose
looking like it's been walked
all over in my sleep.

THE THING ABOUT COURAGE

the thing about courage is --
it's free.

the thing about courage is --
once obtained, it's a relentless force.

the thing about courage is --
it's capable of catapulting you to places
you only read about going.

the thing about courage is --
once harnessed, you're hooked for life.

the thing about courage is --
the fear you once envisioned
soon reveals itself as a mere mosquito bite.

the thing about courage is --
no one really cares if you have it or not.
except you.

the thing about courage is --
you can share it with others,
stretch it wide cross counties and midways.

the thing about courage is --
the power you capture

will be bigger than any fear you
ever avoided.

the thing about courage is --
it's there, way deep down inside you,
huddled behind your pride and persona,
ready to pounce on your troubles.

the thing about courage is --
it's bigger than religion, bigger than sex,
bigger than money, bigger than hope,
bigger than dope, bigger than us all.

Now, release it from its thorny cage
and watch the world fly beside you.

Rob Azevedo, from Manchester, NH, is a radio host and writer, an award winning filmmaker and columnist, and when not writing poems, he sells air for a living . He has a book out called *Notes From The Last Breath Farm: A Music Junkies Quest To Be Heard.*